Combining Wigs, Weaves & Hair Extensions Made Simple

Shon Stoker

TCC South

Crowley Learning Center

Combining Wigs, Weaves & Hair Extensions Made Simple

Copyright © 2016 by Shon Stoker

WWW.WigMakingMadeSimple.Com

Find us on Instagram

@WigMakingMadeSimple

Table of Contents

Introduction to Wigs, Weaves & Hair Extensions

Wigs, weaves and hair extensions are used by women and men to enhance your natural hair by making your hair appear fuller or longer. These hairstyles can also to protect your natural hair from damage.

Why should you create them for yourself? Only you know the vision that you have in your mind of the way you see yourself. With the assistance of this book you have a reference to create the hair you've been dreaming of and save thousands of dollars in the process!

What is a wig? A covering for your head made of human or synthetic hair. With so many advancements in wig making there are a variety of wig caps that offers versatility of styles and methods of attachment for wigs.

What is a weave? A weave typically consist of braiding the entire head or a portion of your hair and sewing hair wefts to your natural hair.

There are a variety of ways hair can be weaved into your hair. For this book we will cover the traditional hand sewing method.

What are hair extensions? Hair extensions can be applied and defined several ways. Most people identify hair extensions in a broad manner. Human or synthetic hair attached to your hair. They can be applied to the hair strand by strand, sewing just like weaving, or with hair clips, micro links, tape or adhesive. Hair extensions can be used to describe weft hair as well, which is mostly how it will be referenced in this book.

Wig Caps, Weaving Nets & Hair Selection

Before creating your wig you must decide which cap will give you your desired results. There are a variety of wig making and weaving caps available on the market now. If you will be combining the wig and weave then you have to choose what weaving net or cap will suite your needs.

The difference in the caps and weaving net is the elasticity and shape. Some caps offer more elasticity than others. The elasticity can sometimes help the cap or net fit more comfortably for longer wear. In my book "Wig Making Made Simple" the caps are different but have the same characteristics. The caps below are the main caps used for this book, however there are new wig caps and weaving nets being created and available at your local beauty supplies periodically. My biggest suggestion is try as many different caps as you desire until you find the cap or caps that work best for you.

Wig Caps

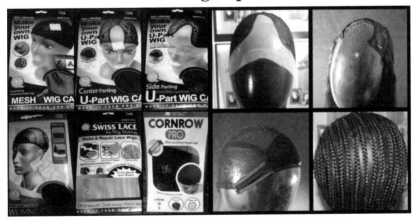

Types Of Hair

Synthetic Hair

Synthetic hair is composed of fine plastic fibers known as low grade acrylic that is heated and strung into strands to make individual hair fibers. Synthetic hair also comes blended with human hair for low grade heating for curling etc. Most synthetic hair comes texturized which is why it is my favorite. Synthetic hair holds curls or waves better than human hair.

High quality synthetic hair is hard to detect that the hair isn't human because of the quality. Synthetic hair can usually be worn straight out the box because it is already styled. The fibers used allow the hair to bounce back in place with minimal effort.

Synthetic hair is less durable than human hair. With proper care synthetic wigs and hair pieces can last up to six months. This hair can cost a fraction of what human hair can cost, making it the most affordable hair on the market.

Human & Synthetic Hair

Human hair offers the most natural look and feel.

Human hair lasts longer and offers the most versatility for styling or coloring your hair. There are different grades and processing methods for human hair. The costs of human hair extensions can vary because of this.

Human hair also requires periodic maintenance, daily styling.

At some point all the human hair extensions matt and tangle eventually, especially if you are bleaching the hair or processing it. So choose human hair wisely.

Both hair types are a good choice depending on your budget, time and needs. You may want to keep both on hand because they both have their pros and cons.

Creating Your Own Hair Wefts

Creating your own custom hair wefts offer a variety of benefits. You can create custom colors or fuller hair wefts. Weft hair is hair that is sewn together into a track system of which secures the root end of the hair together. The weft can be sewn to a wig cap to create your desired wig or it may be used for applying hair extensions or weaving.

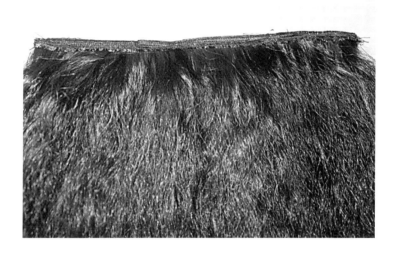

. HAND-MADE WEFT HAIR TECHNIQUE

Tools Needed:
Bulk Hair
Scissors
Sheer Black Ribbon
Sewing Machine
Thread

How to Make Hair Wefts:

Step 1. Set up the sewing machine and thread the machine.

Single Needle or Double needle- Set stitch to zig zag. Stitch tension between 8 and 9. Stitch width set at 2. Stitch length set at .5.

Step 2. Cut your ribbon to the desired length

Step 3. Carefully place hair on the ribbon. Begin slowly sewing the bulk hair to the ribbon. Continue adding the hair to the ribbon.

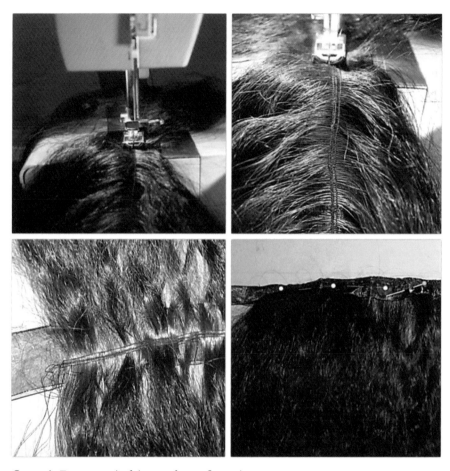

. **Step 4**. Repeat stitching at least four times.

Step 5. Fold the ribbon over and zigzag stitch close to the edge.

Step 6. Straight stitch the edge and below the zigzag at least 3 times.

Step 7. Cut excess ribbon.

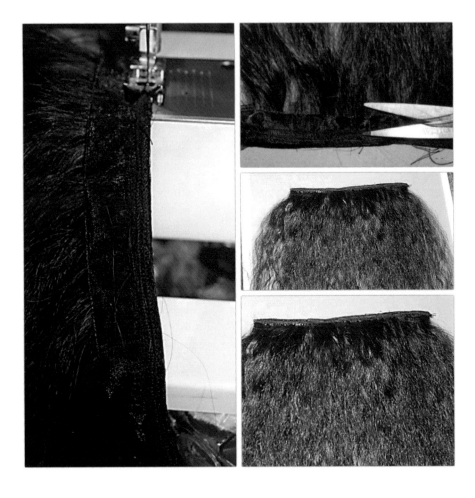

Install your custom hair wefts.

Hair Prepping & Sewing Technique

When sewing hair extensions to your head it important to create a strong foundation to sew the hair too. There are several ways to create a foundations but the simplest is cornrow braids. You can braid the entire head or specific parts of your hair where you want to add the hair extensions.

How to Sew Hair to Your Wig or Your Cornrow Braids
<u>Tools</u>
Shampoo & Conditioner
Hair Wefts
Sewing Needle
Black Thread
Synthetic Hair

Step 1. Prep your hair. (Wash & Condition)

Step 2. Braid the entire head in cornrow braids. Be sure not to make the braids too small or too big. Medium sized cornrow braids work best when sewing the entire head. The cornrow braids will serve as the "anchor" on which the hair extensions will be sewn to. (You can add synthetic hair to the cornrow braids.)

. **Step 3.** Thread your needle and measure your weft hair to cover the area where you want to attach the weft hair.

Step 4. Insert the needle through the hair weft, creating a diagonal stitch all the way to the end of the hair weft, then return in the opposite direction crossing the stitches. (Repeat until you have added all the desired hair wefts to your head.

Machine Sewing Your Wigs

Sewing machines not only can create clothing but wigs as well. Using a sewing machine to sew your wigs takes less time than hand sewing and can be very convenient. However you need to be familiar with the sewing machine to complete a wig using a sewing machine.

Tools

Threaded Sewing Machine

Hair Wefts

Wig Cap

Pin Needles

Scissors

Ventilated Lace

How to Sew Your Wigs with a Sewing Machine

Step 1. Set and thread your sewing machine. Measure your weft hair and place the hair on the cap starting at the back and begin sewing.

Pins can be helpful in ensuring the hair wefts remain in place.

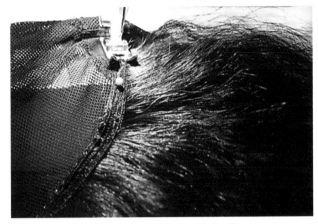

Step 2. As you continue to sew the hair wefts be sure to stretch the cap as you are sewing to ensure that when you are finished the cap will properly stretch over your head.

Step 3. As you work closer to the top of the cap use thinner hair wefts.

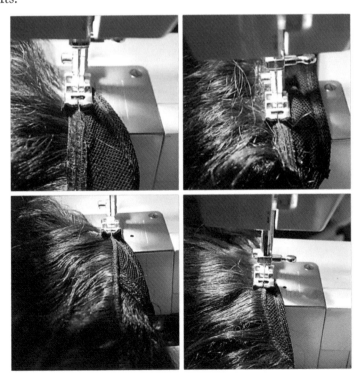

Step 4. Measure and cut ventilated lace.

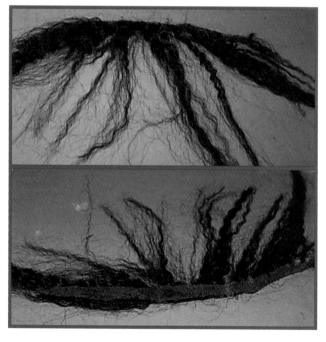

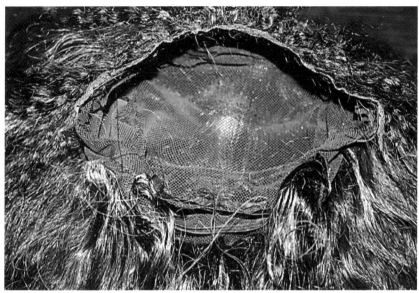

Step 5. Sew the lace around the front perimeter.

Creating Your Own Hair Closures

Creating your own hair closure can save you money and can assist you in creating your custom look. You can create a variety of different hair closures using these basic techniques.

Tools
Swiss Lace or Hair Weave Netting
Hair Wefts
Pin Needles
Threaded Sewing Machine
Scissors
Holding Spray

Step 1. Begin sewing the hair in a circular motion.

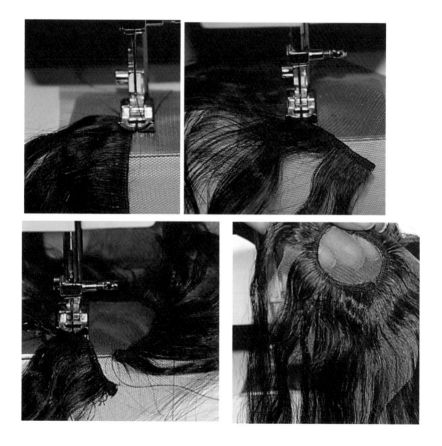

Step 2. Continue to slowly make the circle smaller.

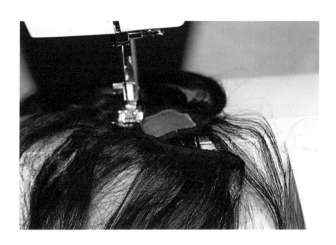

Step 3. Make the circle hole as small as you can but leave a little hole in the circle.

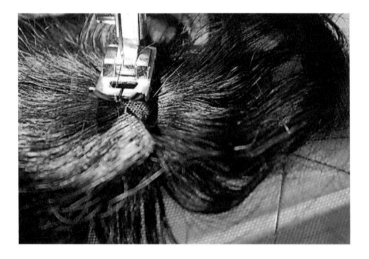

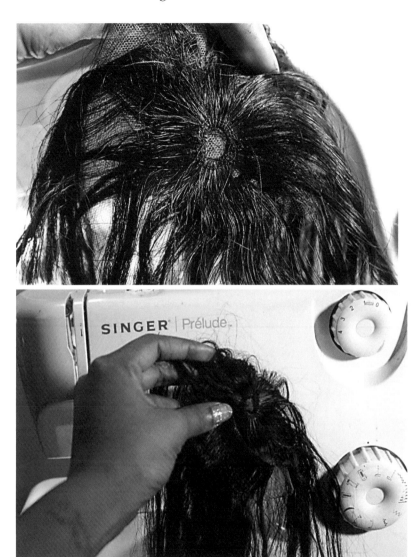

Step 4. Cut a piece hair the length of your index finger and begin sewing it to the small hole.

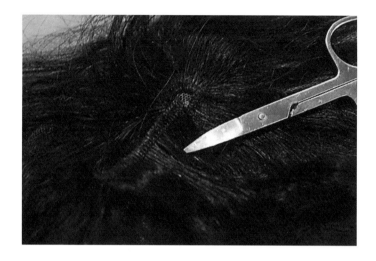

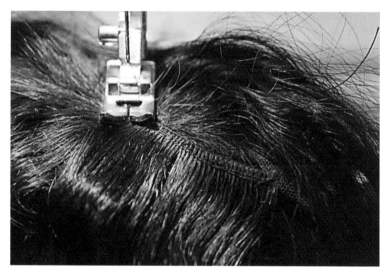

Step 5. Roll the remaining hair into a tight circle.

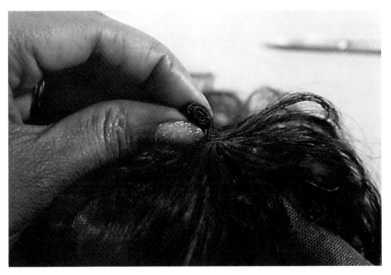

Step 6. Cut a small hole in the closure and push the hair through the circle.

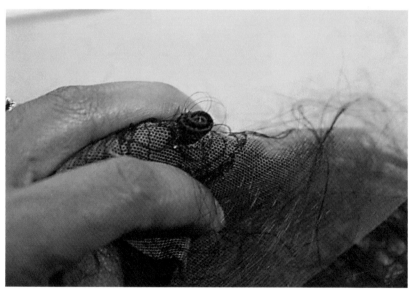

Step 7. Sew the hair to the lace to secure the hair.

Step 8. Spread the hair evenly for proper coverage; add hair spray and you can use your curling iron to assist the hair to stay in place.

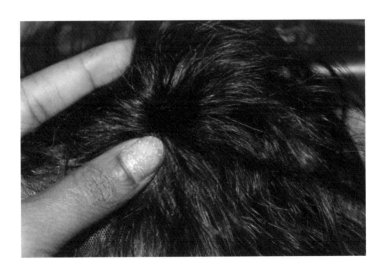

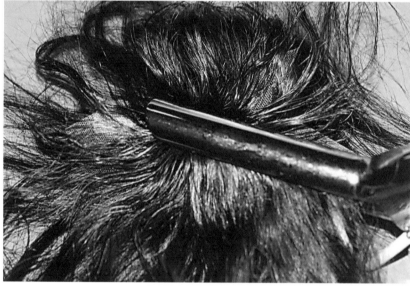

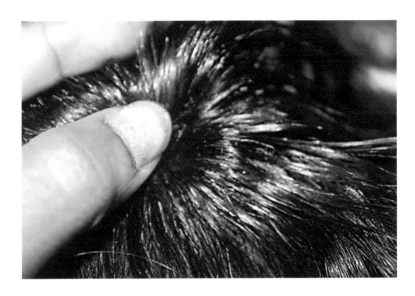

Invisible Lace Closure

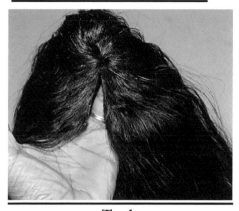

Tools

Swiss Lace

Hair Bonding Glue

Threaded Sewing Machine

Scissors

Hair Wefts

Threaded Hair Weaving Needle

Step 1. Pin hair to lace in a half circle and begin sewing the hair to the lace.

Step 2. Repeat sewing the hair in a circular motion until you have a small half circle.

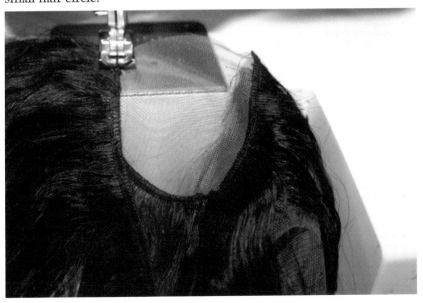

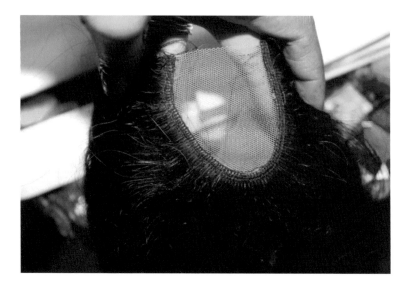

Step 3. Measure and cut hair to place at the front of the lace where the hair meets. You can glue or either sew this hair to the lace. Continue until you have a small hole left.

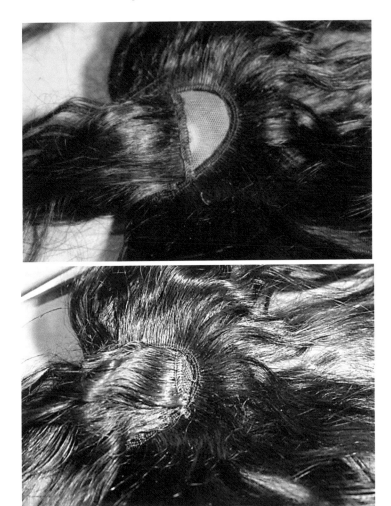

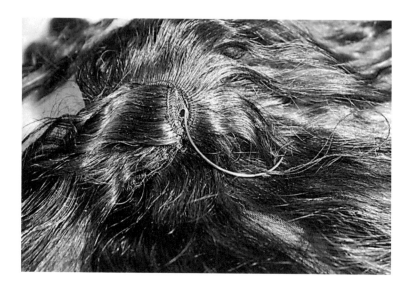

Step 4. Cut a piece of hair the size of your index finger, add glue to the hair and roll the hair into a small circle and push it through the hole.

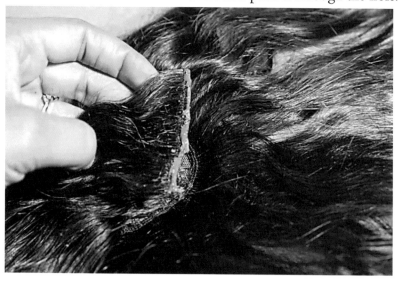

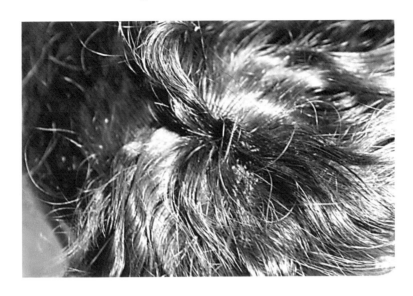

Step 5. Sew the small circle of hair to the lace.

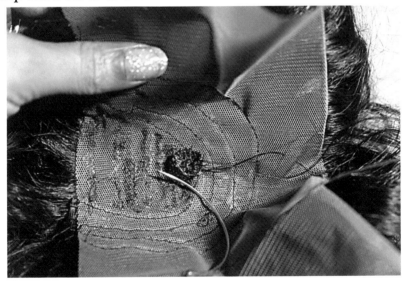

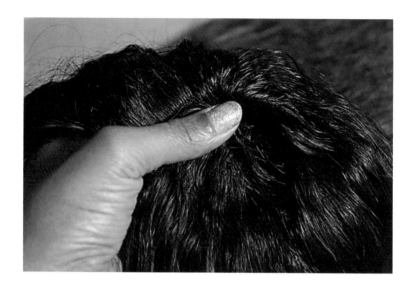

Step 6. Comb the hair out in the front and cut and the hair down the middle.

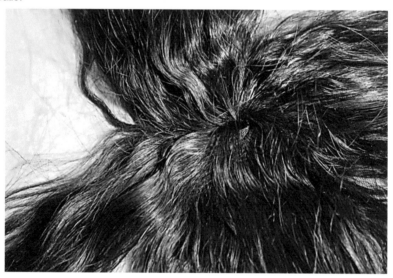

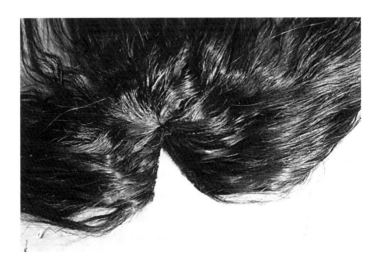

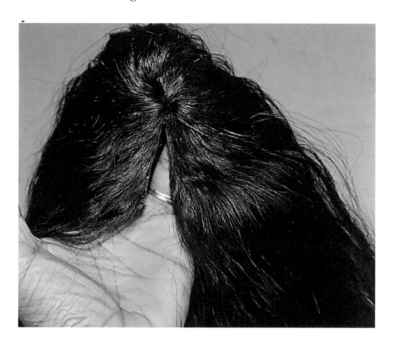

Changing Synthetic Hair Texture

Synthetic hair comes texturized, however you can change synthetic hair texture it's very easy and can help to lengthen the life of your synthetic hair.

How to Change Synthetic Hair Texture

<u>**Tools**</u>
Synthetic Hair Wefts or Wig
Boiling Water
Towel

Step 1. Braid or place the hair in plastic or roll hair into foam rollers.

Step 2. Boil water in a pot and place the hair inside the hot water and remove the hair immediately. (Do not leave the hair inside the hot water.)

Step 3. Unbraid the hair or remove the curlers and now you have changed the texture of synthetic hair.

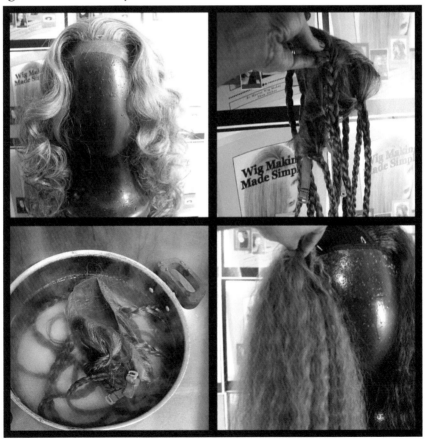

Combining Wigs, Weaves & Hair Extensions

Things to Consider Before Creating Your New Hair
The type of cap you want to use. Calculate how much hair you will need. The amount of hair you'll need depends on the thickness of your own hair and how much length and/or fullness you want to add to your wig or weave. Consider how you'll wear your hair. Think about hairstyles and decide how you want your hair to fall after you have your new hair in place. This is important, as the way the hair is placed dictates how the hairstyle will fall when it is finished.

Basic Tools for Making or Combing Wigs, Weaves & Hair Extensions

<u>Tools Kit</u>
Wig Making Head
Wig Caps
Weaving Caps
Weaving Nets
Human or Synthetic Hair
Swiss Lace
Lace Frontals
Ventilating Needles
Glue Gun
Glue Sticks
Hair Bonding Glue
Scissors
Sewing Machine
Wig Brush

Rat Tail Comb
Wide Tooth Comb
T-Wig Pins
Hair Weaving Needles
Hair Weaving Thread

Creating wigs using different wig caps.

Follow these steps below as a basis for creating all wigs. Start attaching the hair to the back of the wig caps or foundations and work your way to the front of the cap of foundation.

Step 1.   Mount your cap to the wig head using T-Wig pins.

Step 2. Begin sewing your hair wefts to the back of your wig cap. Follow the shape of the cap as a basis to follow or place wefts where you want the hair to lay.

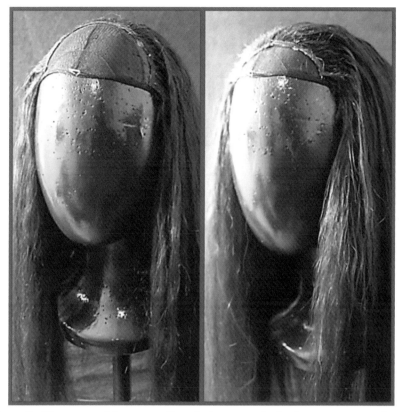

Step 3. You can either ventilate hair around the lace or use a front closure piece.

Step 4. Sew the ventilated lace around the front perimeter.

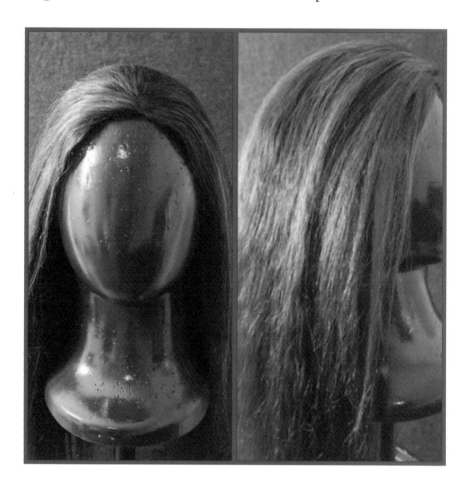

Weaving hair into your hair.

Step 1. Wash and condition your hair.

Step 2. Part and braid the hair into cornrows to create a strong foundation to attach the hair wefts to. (Use synthetic braiding hair to make the cornrows stronger and to protect your hair.

Step 3. Sew the ends of the braid in between the cornrows.

Step 4. Sew the weaving net to your head.

Step 5. Begin attaching the hair wefts to your head using the same technique used in creating your wigs. Begin from the back of the head and work your way to the front of the head.

Step 6. Attach your closure. You must decide where you want the part to be placed and then sew the closure to the head to secure it.

(Follow Previous Wig Making Steps)

Step 1. Beginning from the back of the cap, sew the hair to the formation you want the hair to fall.

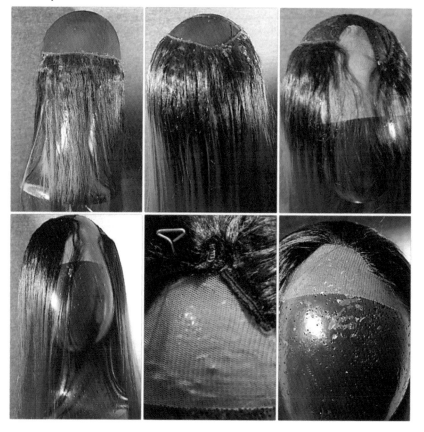

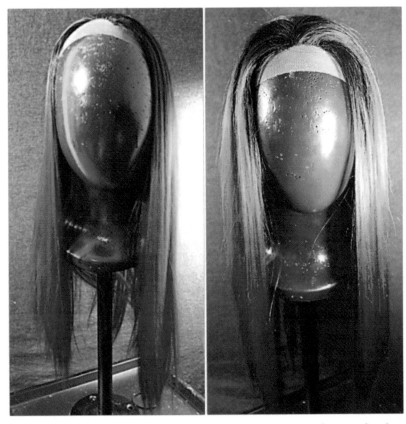

Step 2. Ventilate hair to the front of the cap. (Refer to the book "Wig Making Made Simple" for step by step ventilating instructions.)

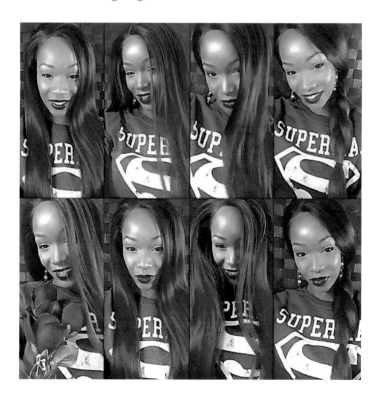

(Follow Previous Wig Making Steps)

Step 1. Mount and cut the wig cap at the back to loosen the tightness of this cap.

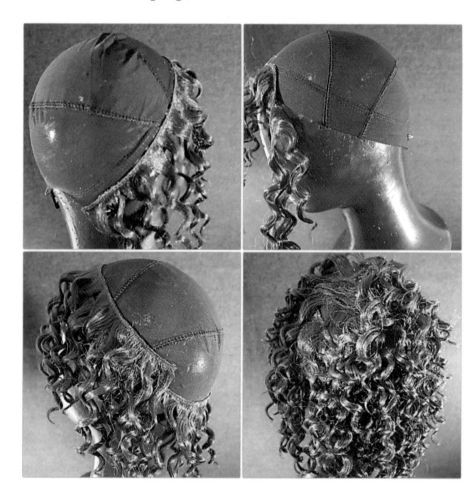

Step 2. Using your glue gun, begin gluing the hair wefts in a circular motion to the cap.

Step 3. Continue the circular pattern and create an extremely small circle and close off the top or create a closure to complete the wig.

(Follow Previous Wig Making Steps)

(Follow Previous Wig Making Steps)

Using this previous wig created you can create another wig with a totally different look!

. **Step 1.**Remove the front closure.

Step 2. Re-texturize the hair.

Step 3. Cut lace front from another wig.

Step 4. Sew the front lace to the wig cap.

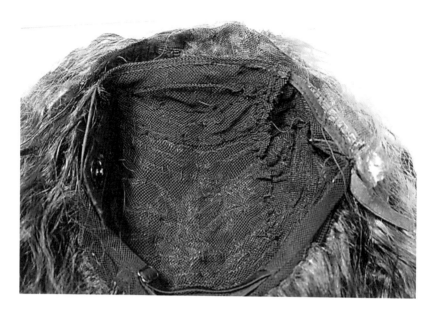

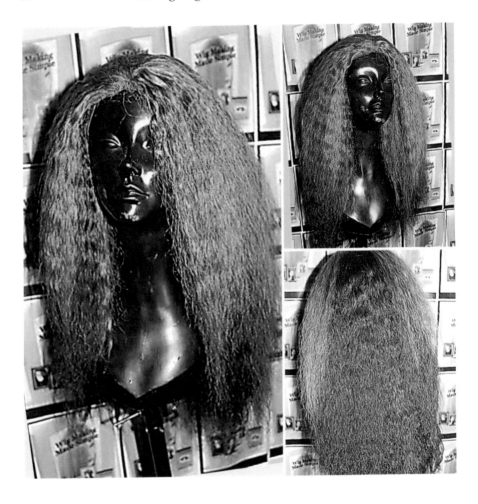

(Using a Pre-Braided Wig to Enhance Hair Fullness)

Step 1. Using a pre-braided wig sew ventilated lace to the front.

Step 2. Using synthetic braiding hair begin braiding the hair, box braid style. Continue to add hair until you feel the hair is full to your liking.

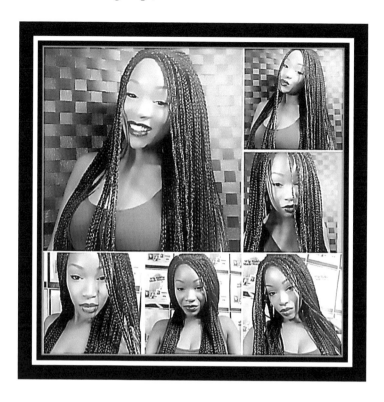

(Adding Hair to Your Premade Wigs)

Step 1. Decide the lengths and colors of hair you want to add.

Step 2. Sew the hair to the wig cap.

Step 3. Style as Desired.

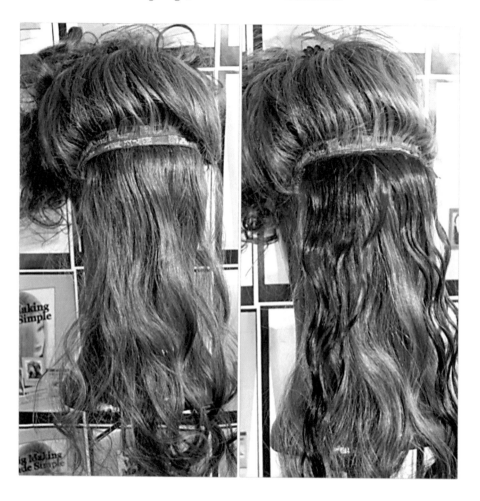

(Follow Previous Wig Making Steps)

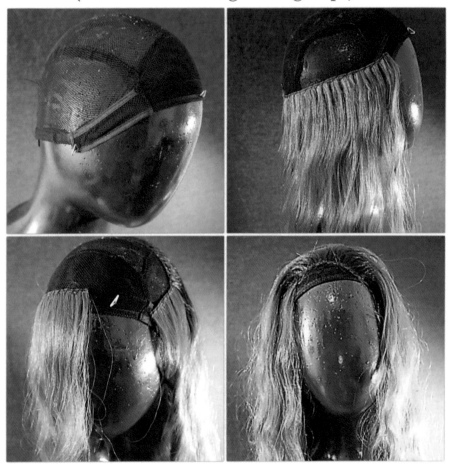

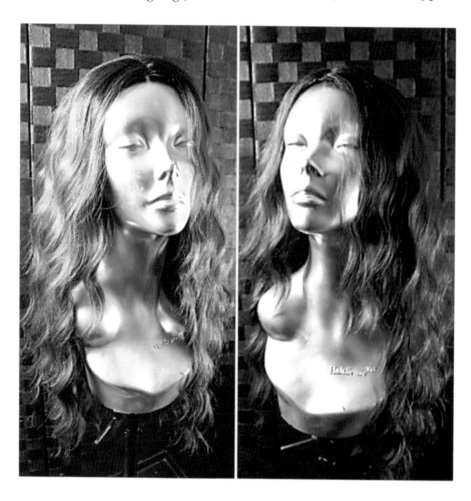

(Follow Previous Wig Making Steps)

(Follow Previous Wig Making Steps)

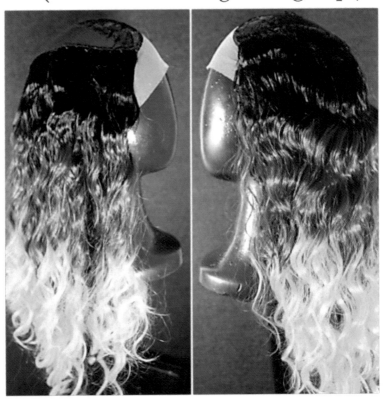

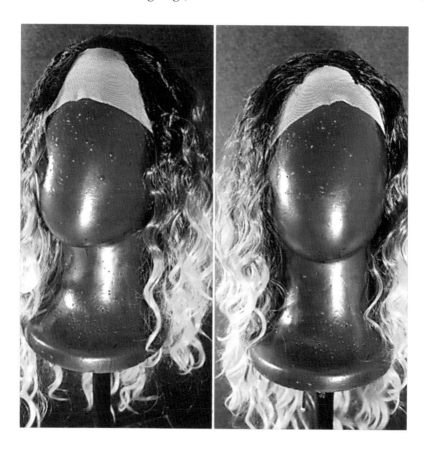

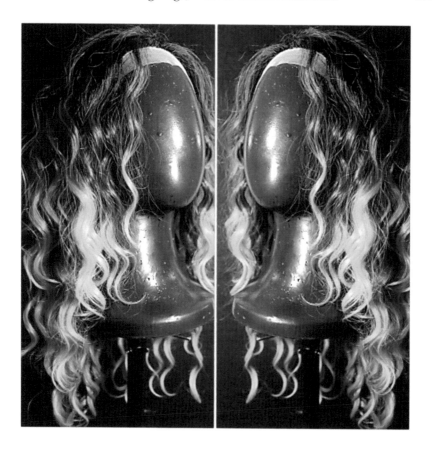

(Re-texturize Synthetic Hair & Create a New Wig

Follow Previous Wig Making Steps)

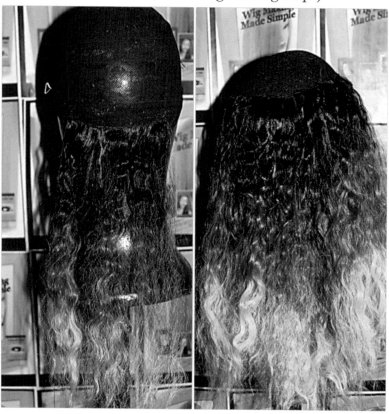

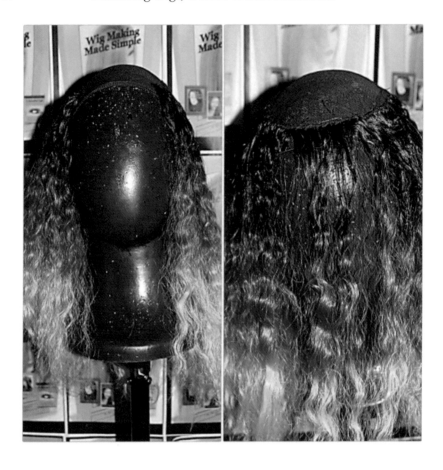

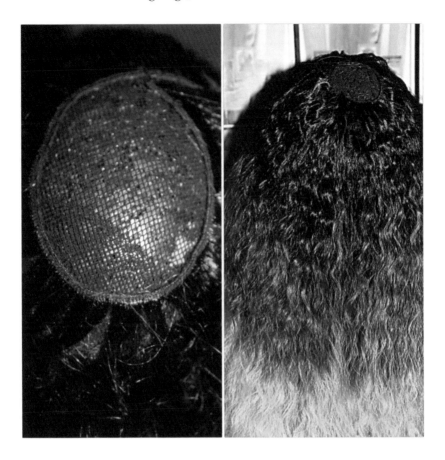

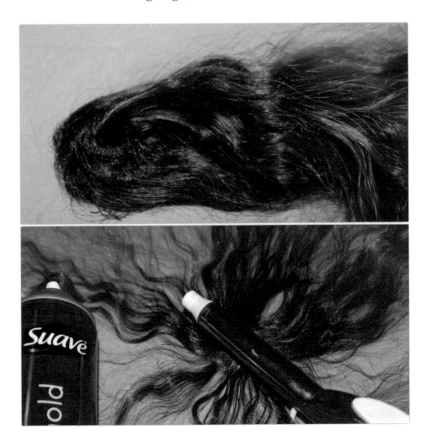

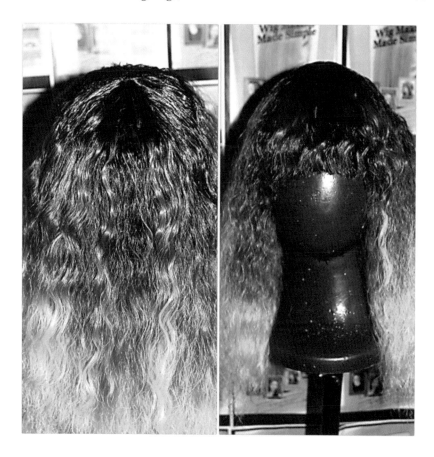

(Follow Previous Wig Making Steps)

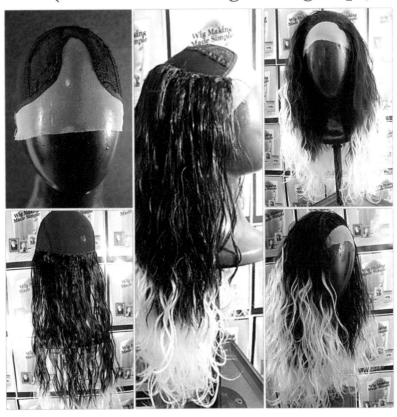

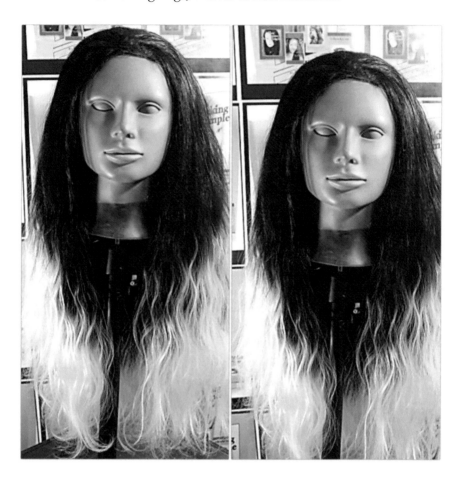

(Follow Previous Wig Making Steps)

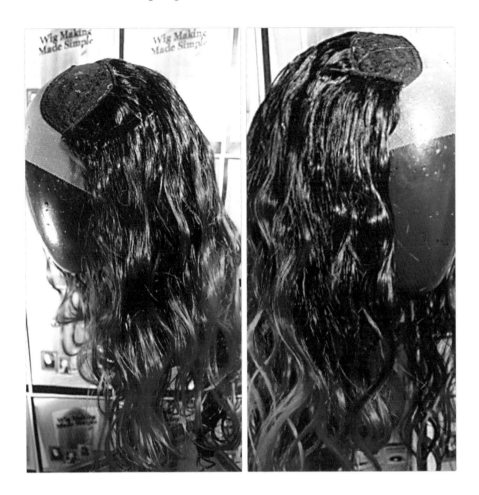

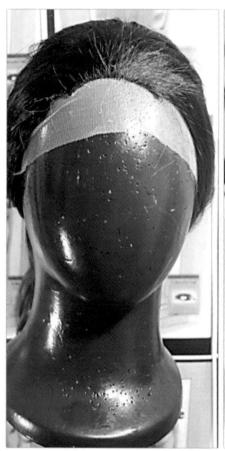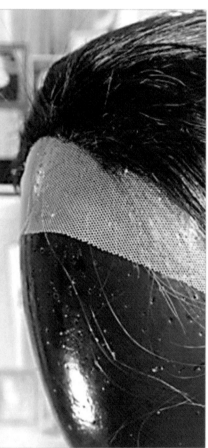

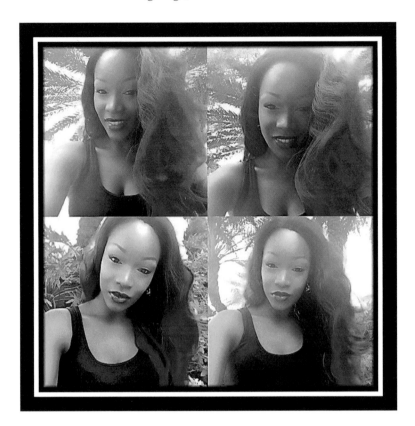

(Re-texturize Synthetic Hair, Cut & Style to Create a New Wig) Follow Previous Wig Making Steps

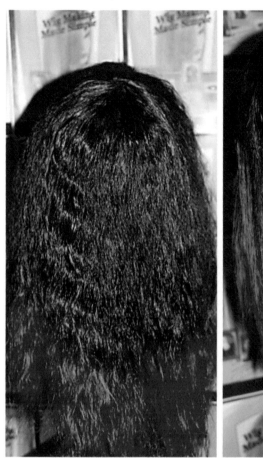

(Follow Previous Wig Making Steps)

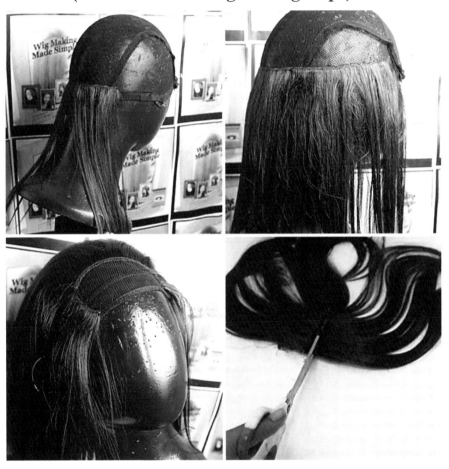

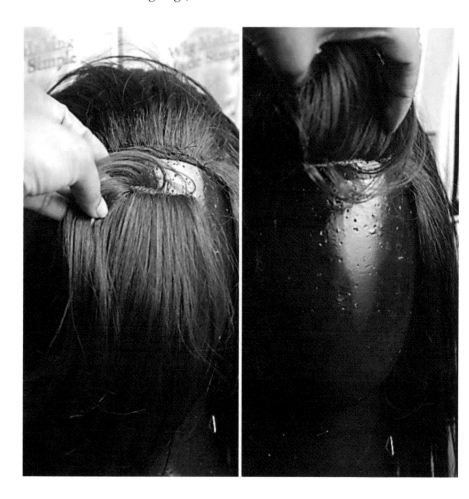

Safe Hair Attachment Technique

Snap Button Hair™

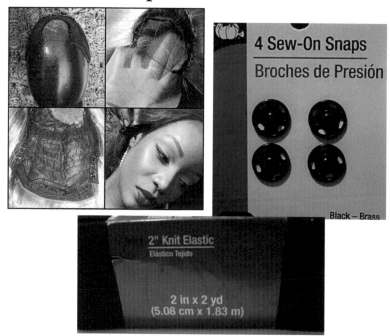

Step 1. Sew elastic to the inside of you lace or wig. (You can choose any size elastic band that is most comfortable to you.)

Step 2. Apply gorilla glue or you can sew on your button to the ends of the elastic.

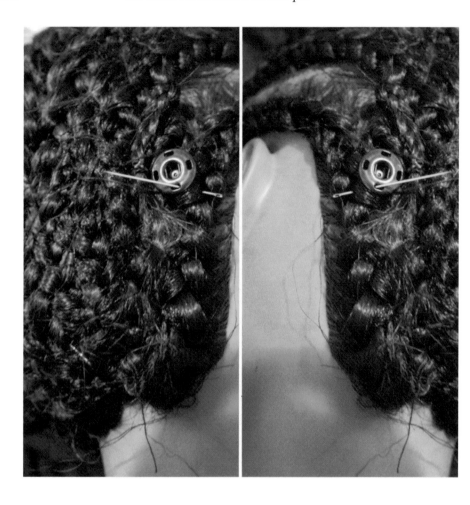

Step 3. Sew the button back to your hair.

Step 4. Attach your frontal or wig.

(You can also add a comb to the front for extra grip and support.)

Snap Button Hair™

Creating Hair Art & Fantasy Looks

Creating hair art and new looks for yourself, simply takes a few tools and your creative imagination.

Hair Art

Decide what the purpose of your hair art will be and gather your supplies. Your supplies are totally up to you because it depends on what your idea is on what you want your hair art to look like.

Here Are Some of My Tools
Glue Gun

Head Bands

Glue Sticks

Seashells

Beads (Accessories of any kind you wish to decorate your hair art with)

Feathers

Step 1. Using your glue gun begin attaching shells to your headband.

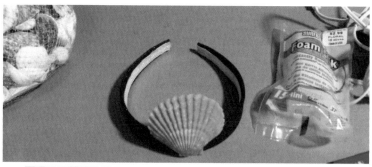

Step 2. Continue to add shells all around.

Step 3. Add any embellishments or jewels you desire,

(Follow Previous Hair Art Steps)

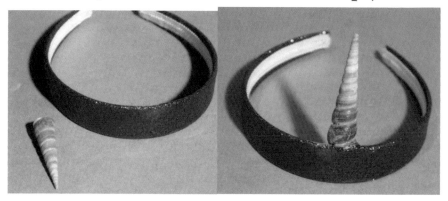

Feathered Headdress

Step 1. You can use any head band, I will be using an extra new year head band. Cut off the top and remove the ruffled paper.

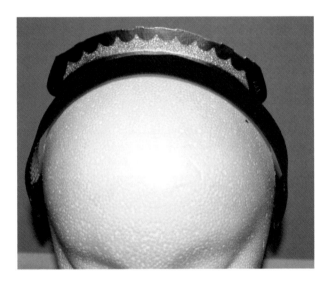

Step 2. Cut a piece of poster paper into a medium half circle and glue it to the top of the headband.

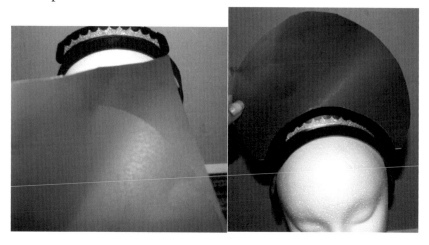

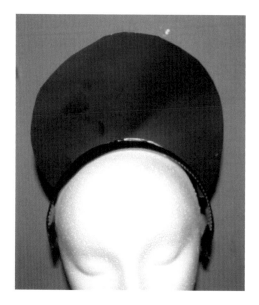

Step 3. Using your glue gun, glue the feathers the front of the headband. Follow any color pattern you desire.

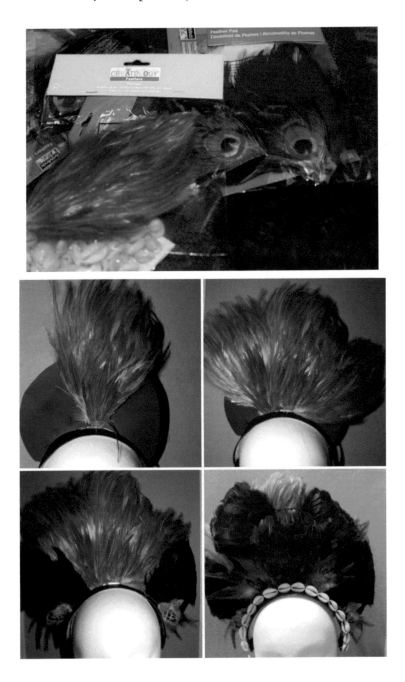

Step 4. Glue cowrie shells around the front perimeter of the headband. (Or any shells or beads you desire.)

Egyptian Crown

Step 1. Cut and glue poster board in circular like cone.

Step 2. Glue twist braid hair around the poster board to create an Egyptian like headdress.

You can add jewels to the headdress if you desire.

Hair Hat

Step 1. Cut and size the wig or hair wefts you will be using to fit the hat.

Step 2. Sew the hair to the inside of the front perimeter of the hat.

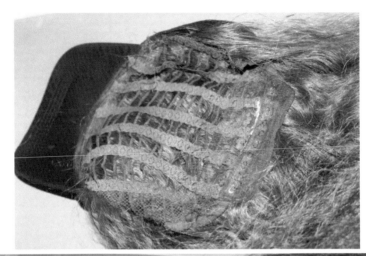

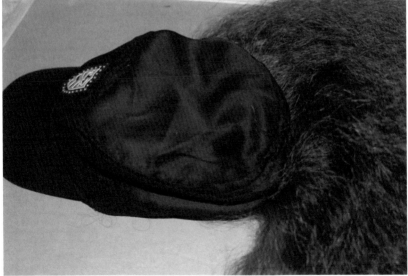

Using Custom Hair Wefts

Step 1. Measure and sew the hair wefts to the inside back of the hat.

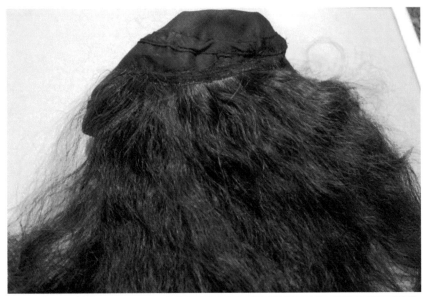

Sporty Visor Hat

Step 1. Sew the hair wefts to the hair net.

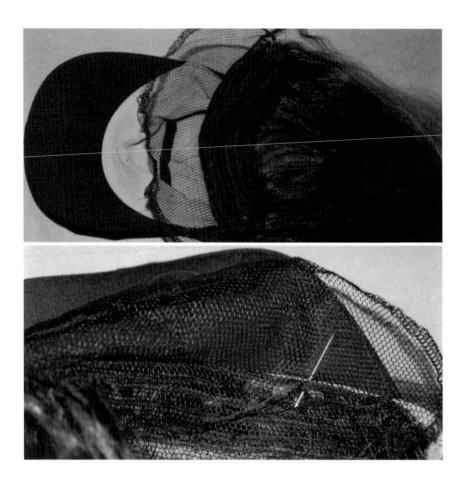

Step 2. Sew the hair to the front perimeter of the cap.

Pompadour Ponytail

Step 1. Using your glue gun, glue the hair in an upward motion.

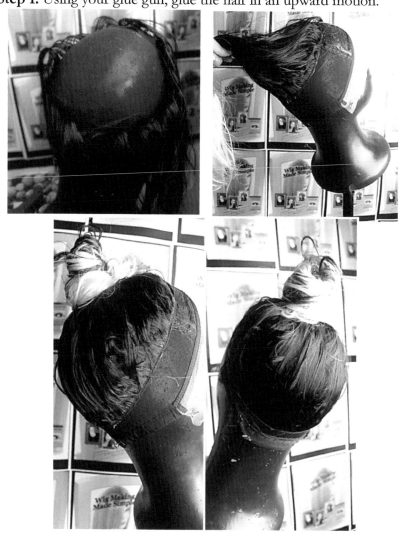

Step 2. Glue closure to the front of the cap.

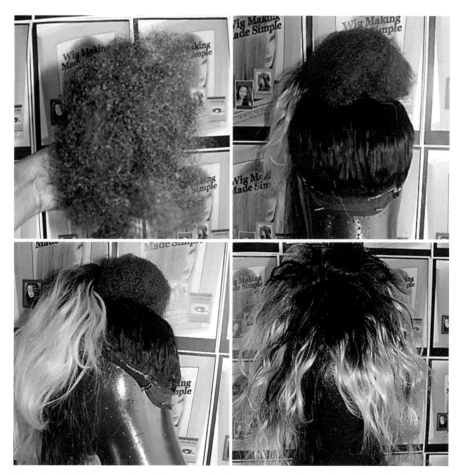

Step 3. Fluff out and roll into a circle some synthetic braiding hair to create a puff to place under the ponytail.

Step 4. Tease the hair and comb it over the hair puff. Use hair spray to hold the hair in place.

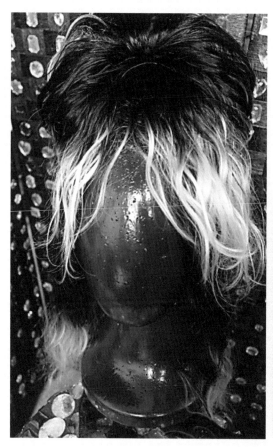

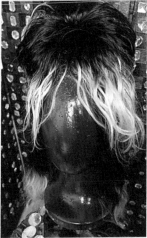

Fantasy Looks (Mermaid)

Tools

Ribbon
Hair Wefts
Sewing Machine
Scissors
Wig Cap
Ventilated Lace

Step 1. Cut ribbon, measure your hair to begin creating thicker hair wefts. Use your sewing machine to sew the hair wefts to the ribbon. (Sew at least three wefts to the ribbon.)

Step 2. Cut excess ribbon from hair wefts.
Step 3. Follow previous wig making steps.

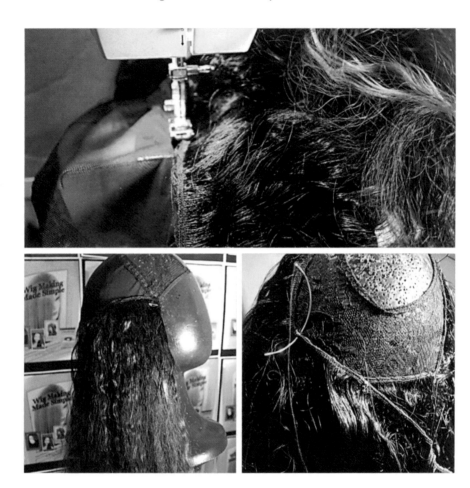

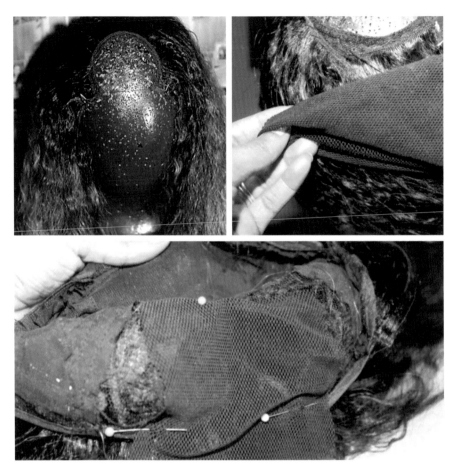

Step 4. Attach weaving net to front of cap.

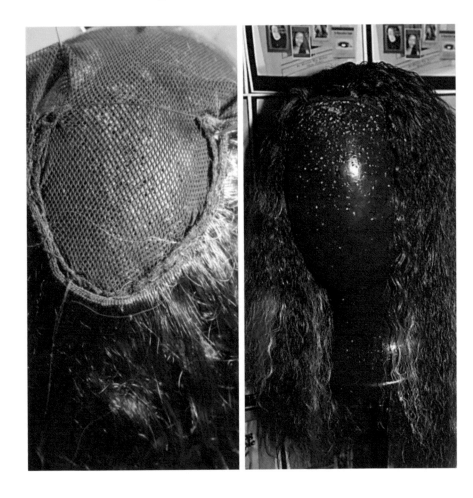

Step 5. Sew hair wefts to top of net.

Step 6. Cut a piece of ventilated lace and add it to the front perimeter of the cap.

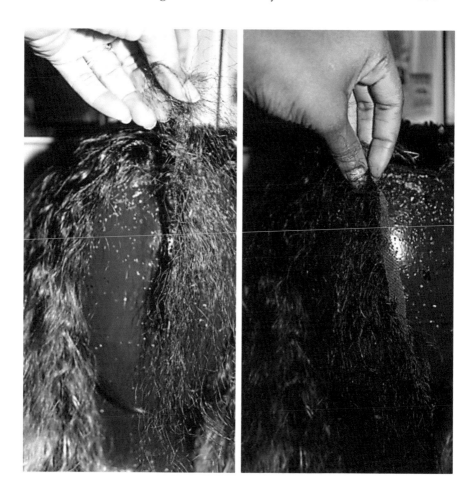

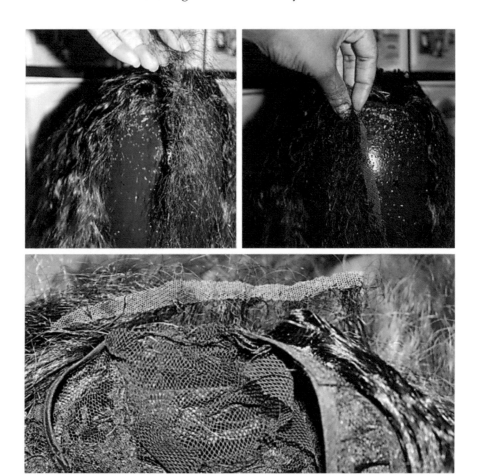

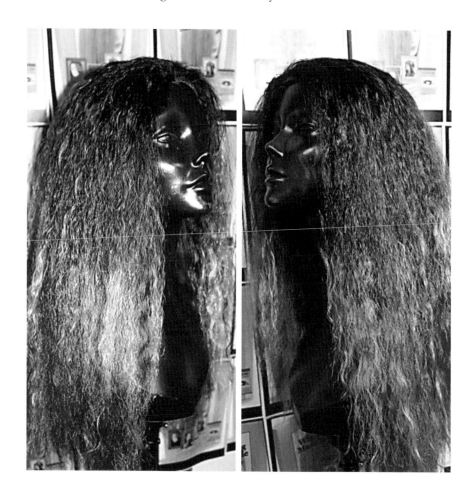

Egyptian Queen

(Follow Previous Wig Making Steps)

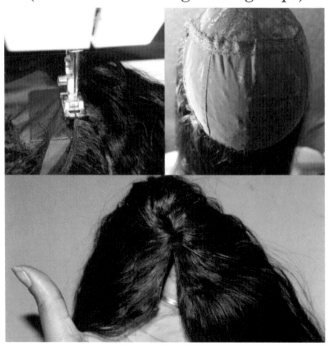

Add previous made closure to cap.

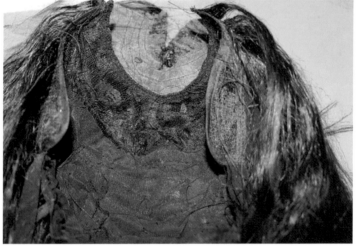

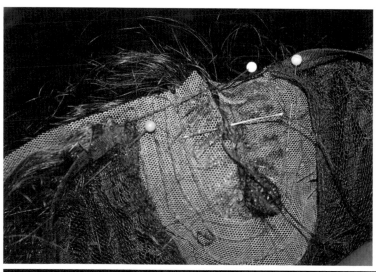

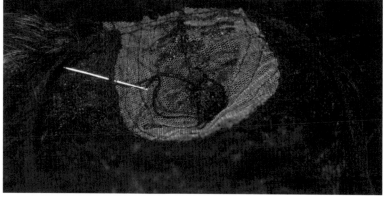

Geisha Girl

Step 1. Remove front closure from previous wig and sew another piece of hair net to the front of the wig cap.

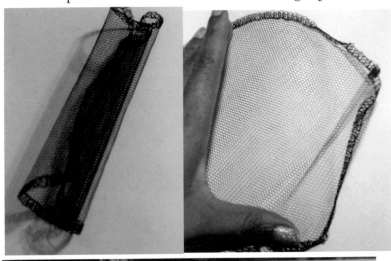

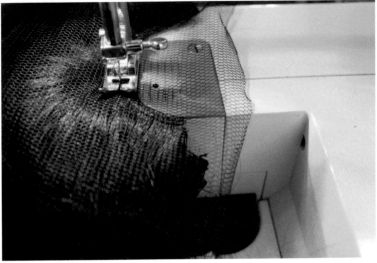

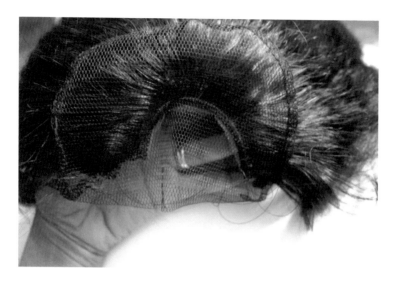

Step 2. Follow previous steps to sew hair to net and ventilated lace to perimeter.

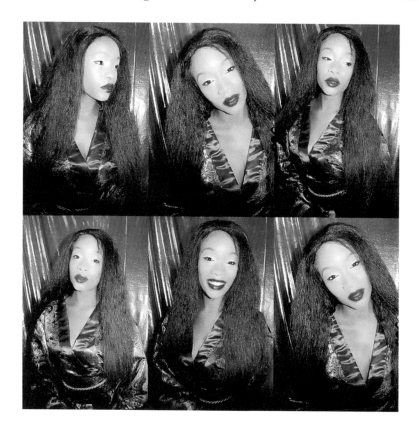

(Follow Previous Wig Making Steps)

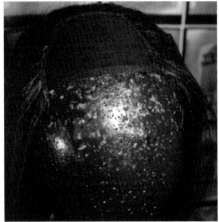

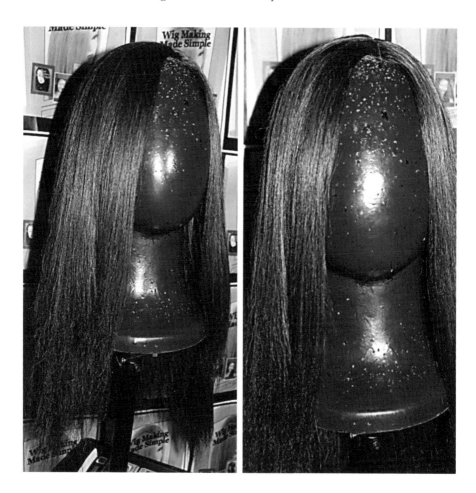

(Follow Previous Wig Making Steps)

CPSIA information can be obtained at www.ICGtesting.com
Printed in the USA
LVIW01n1550060317
526285LV00008B/104